murmur in the inventory

erica lewis

murmur
in the
inventory

Shearsman Books

First published in the United Kingdom in 2013 by
Shearsman Books
50 Westons Hill Drive
Emersons Green
BRISTOL
BS16 7DF

Shearsman Books Ltd Registered Office
30–31 St. James Place, Mangotsfield, Bristol BS16 9JB
(this address not for correspondence)

www.shearsman.com

ISBN 978-1-84861-238-9

Acknowledgements
Portions of *murmur in the inventory* have appeared in the following publications: *Little Red Leaves* (section one), *New American Writing* (excerpts from section five), *With+Stand* ("it starts from what you don't know"), *Word For/Word* (excerpts from sections two and three), *Parthenon West Review* ("think of this as tragic," "this is also true," "people search out the ghosts they find"), *Critiphoria* ("life is not a personal thing," "there is a third dimension to the story," "look at your hands"), and *Ping Pong* (excerpts from section five). A chap project featuring portions of *murmur in the inventory* was published by Ypolita Press.

Many thanks to those editors for their support.

Additional thanks to Norma Cole, Ariel Goldberg, and Rob Halpern.

contents

for mark:
thank you for living with me and my ghosts

An inventory is literally a list of what is found or encountered, from the Latin *invenire*, to come upon. But in the age of "everything at the edge of everything," with "things not lasting at all," inventory itself becomes a shadow, a blur, an impossibility. The crisis of infinite worlds: how could anyone catalog the encounters of even one hour of one day on Facebook, Twitter, Google, the Internet? erica lewis is a poet or eulogist of memory, who seeks in the materiality of body a language that could make the present persist beyond the nanomoments we increasingly exist within.

Our bodies are "forever recomposing" in these pages. As the poems accumulate and aggregate, meaning shimmers in a nacreous between, a "dislocated cloud" of fragments that would suture us: body to body, person to person, life to life. The poems drive to our hardnesses—bones, teeth, nails—to insist that amid all the sloughing off of history and experience we still are built of something solid, and that we are "going to have to scream that it hurts," all this loss. And while we are left ghosts of ourselves, in separate existences, the shadows and murmurs that erica lewis weaves together in this courageously beautiful book chase "the memory / of our sacred" with a fierce love that will reach out and grab you.

—Dan Thomas-Glass

------------------------margin or error or understanding
as if we had been better all along portraying fragments

one

----------------------------------in this separate existence was a shape

you are still here where i left you

you are your own ghost

----------------------------------i liked the memory of the arrangement

unsupported in this space of only you

how

to use place as substitute

this law of reserved effort

------------------------------------that most things we are drawn to only because
they are familiar

jotted on the back of photographs

the things that trouble us

that often linger

some old advice

floats to the surface

that lullaby

the back of a photograph

people say i'm crazy but i believe that you just have to

live with the things

the juxtaposition

in what you don't see

the great hot emptiness ahead

what you keep calling memory

-------------------------------------to shrug off

the urgency

we wean ourselves from ourselves

----------------------------------the secret of the straying
and straying is its flight into the strange
in the midst of the familiar

the very clear

sense of aching

awareness of how far short

need is an ending is an analysis

fragments from the metal

the low spark

spaces trying to get out etc. etc.

how particles accumulate
how we particle reveal and then the particular

distance is not something you believe in

and yet you are so far from yourself

the wind

the dust

you know this isn't everything

say it

say it

----------------------------------between

a firework and a reflection

i said water

i mean forever

i touched those eyelids as objects

as captions of brevity

as you know her only as what survives in fragments

i touched those objects

to capture change

throw it away
it may seem less relevant

i don't know why that's why

it's why

the job is to take and tell the stories

-----------------------------------the rip out window
the scaffold holding up your

inadvertent

this spurt response caught in your head

or window your faceted object

like how you have worked and worked lather
now there's a real piece of me

location diffused as linger

you've been drifting again

you say that because there is nothing to remember

so as not in the place

you will need to replace the brakes
to see how you use lonely

------------------------------------the pressure of function

you are the device for some devious spit
the face of
how the imitation of life depicts life

liar

now there is a word

or bust the trap and forget
who you are by name

----

layer upon layer

the outlay of plans

you by your own flaws

a story about a man

about

she likes music
listens to one

jagged edges lapping up brass cement

please knock down please wake up

still lives together
they've all blended

murmur in the inventory

--------------------------------constituent parts

lay down

i keep imagining

--------------------------------this is not for you to use

tried to kick it off

it's a shame you fell

such is modern guilt

that little souvenir

for if you throw darts at the songs

----------------------------------a memory from someone else
forms a character
there is no back

buckets of rain
will happen today

as it existed in the last place

there are no particulars

and locations
we measure ourselves by

walls as cold as a gallery

where the story ends

what cannot be taken away

think of you
humming in that house of cards

----------------------------------i am not coming back

i am never coming back

it looks like more than it really is

------------------------------he decided to beautify myself with his feathers

a bird shaped you shaped absence

in the air

a flutter by

turns white and black

flicker speaks where about an object

you have been falling for months now

banking on the oldest story in the book

----------------------------to burn yourself out with the try

how you should unpack when you stay

call it watch or visit

i do it most in the static

to scatter how the mess wills

to happen

------------------------------------i wanted to mark this moment very clearly

were you able to have
a hand and an empty pocket

what would you
place upon the table

but he didn't say anything about it

he kept it to himself

----------------------------------in my head i am the passenger

teller of tall tales

everything on the edge of everything

------------------------------------busy with shadows
even in the afternoon

they seem to freeze a moment
goes in circles

jotted on the back of

what you keep calling memory

sough

i'm not here for you to blow on

two

----

i was there

another person or another life

strange how one can

disassociate the days

when it separates
i owe you one or one

tarnished what you keep

locked in the basement

the lip of your glass

on the table

to tell you about it

keep your eyes shut

unimportant what passes between
one is one's own

misrecognition

read as an epigraph

an empty room of something sparse

-------------------------------------we live in a place of corridors
it is true and not real
and you turn the corner

framing light referends

slowly
and disperse as equal impermanence

of waves

white lines

who had once played for the silents

but he didn't think

they'll heat to vapor

of things not lasting at all

go around me
you know the answers

and real and not true

------------------------------------to record the tension

you're much crazier than the weather

live quietly within this city

and murmurs

and names we can not acquire

but my fingers

had been kept secret

hello

i didn't recognize your face

--------------------------------crosses and recrosses

a landscape of habit

nearly killed me

why did you go

-----------------------------------the answer is no

what the storm removes

talking

your old time religion

these separations

-----------------------------------if you look hard enough
you can see faces in the bark

limb from limb

nobody helps a liar

----------------------------------think of this as tragic

the whole or just one thing

this one

just a tinted

of time gone by

going all aflame and ochre

undetected

her handwriting

a gulp of bracing air

the first few months under the trees

transcendence that goes
like you do

holding himself together

baling wire and duct tape

centimeter by centimeter

a mouthful of spit

then circle back

----------------------------------shape memory

a dislocated cloud

hits the bone

you can't go back

----

mime

asphyxiate

there is no

it made me feel less alone

------------------------------------in the present you reconcile

whatever you want

you think you know

what happened to you

here is where i get the shakes

how the trees imitate trees

how you imitate you

if you stare hard enough

tripwire

strings attached

what remains

if you have to take sides

in his arms like a child

----

hands on the ceiling

it won't replace

right where you would fall

\-where the time goes
what you call retaining

vomit talk

it's not this quiet

some kind of animal

i think last night was

a slip of the tongue

thing

significance

thing

how you keep finding me here

as elephants have past lives

this thing is bigger than you

and to retrieve it

retains of a particular

an empty coat of somebody

lead on my face

them with their kill

----------------------------------soon and soon
it has to

fucking stop

night

an explanation

your eyelashes

jumping into my chest

if you weren't real
i would make you up

every song

i am what

the water

ringing for patterns

still to the count

for nothing forward

----some people may think you're wrong but i know you're onto something
something for something

momentum and so on

illusion

peacock

you exaggerate everything

these breakwater years

what you can't predict

to the bone

stop trying

for a mouth to repeat in

you're going to need somebody

i know

we talk all the time

say it
say it

quid pro quo

i'm counting on your lips

----------------------------------begin at the beginning

don't fit

in my own skin

over and over and over again

three

----

chasing

the memory of

our sacred so and so

i steal everything

to reconstruct air

that something splits into

these bodies lacking parts

make a fist

put your mouth over my mouth

ruins and ghosts

we'll never leave this room

---------------------------------fair enough

keep firing

and though it changes you

i mean to leave everything

thinking i am thinking

already a man without lips

about one thing

i forgot

i forgot i forgot

i know nothing of physics

about putting skin on

how you are attached

to this machine and to its timing

girl you myself as a child

the way it echoes you

is to echo you

now and from the side

no matter what it sounds like

it is the sound of burning

----

the danger is that we will listen

we went looking for lightning

it did me in

----------------------transparency would translate beautifully to the bottles

navigators

little bird

actual black

but these are not my shoes

random unhappiness

backing you up

in faucets

in frames

what you want to remember

don't worry darling

soon and very soon

events call themselves into question

nobody knows nothing

white waxed cocoons

black waxed dioramas

everyday i make up things to take seriously

----

it's not about geography

when the past becomes the now

he is leaning over her from the other side

fraught seams

these beats are twenty years old

if i could be that for someone else

between her stockings and her skin

----------------------------------don't try to change my conviction

a little map

in your mouth

in my mouth

ricochet

by your own memory

a cage of fire things

i want to hear you

i only remember falling

then you must

tell me i'm crazy

you told me i'm

all people inside

i can't drink my coffee until i put you in the closet

close your mouth just close it

you were here last night

you were driving circles

----

tell me would it kill you

not the other way around

glossy red songs

i will find you in the distance

----------------------------------and then there was the other

and then it is a matter of how well we learn to read the signs

how well we are able to manage
how well we are able to maneuver

the presence of these shadows once in a room

warm desperate magnet

memory occurs in the present

as the pendulum somehow making time

and excuses and excuses and excuses

----

these empty themselves

in your chest

the necessity

to be something though there is no other way to be

if i carry your face as water

a body

sifting through the yellowed

in its own skin

in darkness we discovered the pattern

the bones matter

the things we are not going to finish

i forgot

i forgot your face

but it wasn't your face

----

people search out the ghosts they find

the color of water woven without us

how your image stiffens

we staple and turn them upside down

we knew who we were aiming at

we were aiming at ourselves

----------------------------------supposing we could separate the two

there is a hole

a nest alive with

other people

relocation of fragment in you

you were bleeding somewhere

then also something from somewhere else fills you up

----

so it's not forgotten

the horizon pulls a line

i know you'll figure it out

it fell from my pocket

i watched it melting

dear light you are like blood

if you believe

i can give you something

----------------------------------the other's gaze brings you

the baggage for clues

the way that people die

into existence

----

we will be discovered

then we will leave

but that was me

who needed mending

-----------------------------------life is not a personal thing

to sing about an object into place

a floor plan

how you would

change the scale

as when the weight rinses out the burned

firecracker

water

everything white is turning

i did what i needed to do

are you not furious

-----------------------------------there was light and light

until it burns you

four

----

mercury tinted

survival technique

you find love or death as it finds you

----------------------------------i wanted to go outside

us in our seatbelts

but i will do that tomorrow

when i get up

herein lies the absence
a strange garment
in the lines that flicker

yes it always mattered to me more than anything else

----------------------------------this is also true

we were meant to be thinking of love as property

hum with me

do you want to feel my bones

at the glass and the glass

if i promise to carry the small bits

frames a face

of stories that fracture me

the speech is an indication of what we don't hear
necessary avoidance
a violent sly anguished
mocking smoke which keeps
the other in its place when true silence falls
we are left with the echo
we are nearer to nakedness

i carry your face as water

this is why i beg

-----------------------------------if in pieces we are accurate

it would be wrong to call this nostalgia

it's something else which also has to do with remembering

sometimes people are sad to be separated
by a train or window and sometimes
they are relieved
i had intuited that
but there's knowing and knowing and parts of us know things
that won't respond to reason or proof

they make us more numerous in silence

----------------------------------there is a third dimension to the story

it's in the turning of the weathervane

and this has nothing to do with calmness

to get lost in a surface that has no patience

you stand the figures
in a circle and behind
like the bed sheet indentations of someone who has left
each one a person in the light that shines through
each letting flicker as it slips

i was the sea

in the house where the noise started

a thousand miles of it

i forgot

i forgot i forgot

to ask you everything

----------------------------------this is how we got here

the horizon leans forward offering you steps

you simply keep going as the shadows get long

until my eyes were ashes

is an ending is an analysis
separating flesh from bone
the parts of you that die from the parts of you that come back
how the dead and the living go on
talking to each other
patiently telling the same story

the little bones of each

sculpture and sticks and stones

to slip inside the cracks
the pieces that don't fit together so good

say it

say it

that there be nothing finally

------------------------------elsewhere and elsewhere we can almost remember

this is a photograph of real life this is the only chance you have at real life

the place where things are cut

is it enough to have some love
small enough to slip inside a book
small enough to cover with your hand
we know and understand things as we apprehend them through our bodies
and also to bring in other voices as all else breaks down
the pounding of a nail into my forehead as narrative sometimes adheres
to these things
what you keep calling memory
will stop and wake

this

that memory will persist

a body forever recomposing

----------------------------------and what we are beneath right now

trying to view this not as a turn of events but rather a digression back
into structure

you learn to drive
to read history against the grain
you drive all night to find yourself
standing in the road
i realized that against the dark
i don't believe in god i only believe in human beings
but they would say anything to shut me up

back matter

cracked rib

i will stop when it strikes me

i haven't slept in years

--------------------------------to take and tell the stories

my wrists are made of sand

you slice yourself in half

to watch

to absorb the tiniest of ink

fragments bend back on themselves so as not to interfere
with the geometry of all this breathing in and never
breathing out like a stone like they bury the dead to hurry them on
i don't know about specifics i don't know about the world
i am in a cave of sitting
like you and your way with words

eroded

older

and excuses and excuses and excuses

----------------------------------the circumstances in order

say you have died but disclosure doesn't necessarily lead to enlightenment
the more clearly the past is revealed in fact the less the characters seem
to understand one another or themselves it isn't insight that binds them
it's the absence of it

misplace the death

then the severance

it will never rain

five

-----------------------------------it starts from what you don't know

you love the white too just because it's white

a thing to stand in front of fear

but what i sent doesn't talk about the call

we can't help exclaiming at the thinness of our skin

i beat myself up i fly around in circles

you're just fucking up the situations

nothing so sad as someone else's shoes

but we still had miles to go before we slept miles to go

see cracking bones make noise

see you're doing it without me

what was it that burning that endless insufficiency

i remember seeing horses

as a person you can feel and there is a certain humiliation attached to this

call it what you will

taking all that's left and making a parachute

strapped to my chest

it's still no way to behave

but everything that rises must

say it

say it

ballast

so i will hold my own hand

----

look at your hands

in the shape of a tree branch

body steering the mind

out of the way

the force compels the character

makes a zero of things

leaves behind fragments

trumpeting into an empty drain

you see that split between atoms

say i'm bleeding on my own body

but i can't speak outside the things i mean

i mean this place has failed us

states have a history

you gather something you leave something you've been hauling with you behind

it is hard to stumble across a fictitious version of yourself

confusing the movement with the dancing

of course you love the monsters

how the sky turned white how everybody froze

i suffer mornings most of all

relying on signals for comfort

you would feel negative towards a square of paper

but i like the sound of that word kite

we look up to discard the weight

----------------------------------bodies dream of themselves

the accumulation is undeniable

disorder the mess the non-resolutions

those remains in place of my image

you might start with meaning and end up with frequencies

the little piece that came out but not so little

maybe only because the dissonance feels more accurate

the shape we desire changes

along with the need to bury things alive

the past seeping in and seeping in

forms as silent observers

that dirty fallow feeling

it draws you in hopefully

it stays with you

everything very very angular and small

but you see the ebb and flow

wants to knock you out of your complacency

means to an end that refuses you

thing

significance

thing

and so i imagine my image

lines and eventually shape

the lines we made up

the mere act of willing going to pieces

we watch all of this emerging

you suspect it yourself

if you had cared more you would have remembered

----------------------------------at least the acceptance of forgetting

what is not being told not said about us about you in particular

effigies in these circles

circles are endpoints

i wish i knew how to separate the two

but then you just have to take a deep breath and be like it's ok

in the inside there is sleeping

everything fitting together with gravity like a puzzle

the space between bodies between people it hangs from the ceiling

the distinction between soundlessness and sound

things occur things happen things shift

they set me on fire too

so you have to understand the pieties

these words that sound strangely toothless

messy reality has always pressed itself

in images of the people we might become

i have long since lost my hands in the circuitry

i just say to all of them just lead me

wounds beneath the competence show your bones

the area is exposed

i'm sorry

i just want you close

but you are not close

you are just a little bit happier than i am

----------------------------if you help me live through this maybe you can stay

but you could only write about what's inside of you

the burning in your mouth

why it's suddenly so hard to breathe

why a quilt of paper

a nest alive with words

my mouth not spoken by me

memory resolves to nothing but what's upon us

like the men we used to be

bailing wire and duct tape

a sort of fissure left standing there

the way the sun has coppered our faces

like spectres like pilot flames

every now and then

we all just wait for a minute

for things to draw near

i put my wrists in

a little ghost to lick your palm

these lines of thought and fracture

these

which i repeat back

i say them quietly back to you

----------------------------------if you repeat the names they disappear

between water and a line of type

a lump in my throat

blows into the tubes located at your shoulders

the hole in your lip is bleeding

you don't know what to think so i'll tell you

both are true

there are no neutral storms

memory or loss bores holes into you

here's what happened here's what some people say what happened

i can't separate the two

no distinction between fiction and fact no distinction

it's not your fault

you can't see the sutures

so i cross reference the living with someone else's skin

scene from the door scene from the window scene from the inside

my fingers cast a shadow down the center

supposing we could separate the two

shards on your face account for all those references

in someone else's words

the pieces spread thin from intention

oh yes

you should definitely use both hands for that speech

----------------------------------to lineate comes and goes

i no longer remember the exact date only the month and year

there was a rare electrical storm and i just watched it sweep across the sky

a lick around the perimeter and then you forget

maybe the confessional can no longer be confronted head on

but there are rules and then there are methods

maybe i was a dancer all along

history hovers in a deep sleep so that you can't resume

the movement and the spin

there's the thing and then what the thing really means

don't let what the thing means scare you away from the thing ok

the disconnect that turns up i think is an important thing to feel from time to time

memory spitting blood into an enamel basin

how generous you are within your specifications

i'm finding it harder and harder to stay in touch

to weep and laugh at the same time

forms the time that isn't anything yet

and i have so many questions like are you ok

or maybe i better not ask that

we communicate so much worse with all these marbles at our disposal they call it instinct

the space waiting to harden

but you are nothing to me you are like air

firecracker

water

to speak to where the echo is

we take the shape of the thing that moves us

----------------------------------lately i've caught myself feeling

this is a fairytale

better get my shit together better gather my shit

let the ground know who's standing on him

you're in this condition of doubt

you have to throw the right way or you have to let go

you shouldn't be trying to juggle your own fire all the time

such collapsing bleeds under the skin

the body is akin to the conspiracy but because it cannot be rational
this makes it clear it does not matter

time stops and you are reminded that human relationships can be both

simple and unsolvable

the sickness inherent in representation

here have my arms

we go into these things totally blind

an empty page feeling helped by geography

we stop walking we are taking that walk

this thing that's like touching except you don't touch

one foot and one foot

and whatever else this place isn't

but then he was a tourist and a tourist can't help but have a distorted
opinion of a place

i realize myself doing these things

calling it memory

you probably don't even have to imagine chances are you have experienced some degree of reversal yourself

spinning plates to square every process

the room in which a death

we rest on forms assumed

you're going to have to scream that it hurts